CALIFORNIA INTERIORS

CALIFORNIA INTERIORS

JILL COLE

The Library of Applied Design

PBC International · New York

Distributor to the book trade in the United States and Canada:
Rizzoli International Publications Inc.
300 Park Avenue South
New York, NY 10010

Distributor to the art trade in the United States:
PBC International, Inc.
One School Street
Glen Cove, NY 11542
1-800-527-2826 Fax (516) 676-2738

Distributor to the art trade in Canada:
Letraset Canada Limited
170 Duffield Drive
Markham, Ontario L6G 1B5, Canada

Distributed throughout the rest of the world:
Hearst Books International
105 Madison Avenue
New York, NY 10016

Library of Congress Cataloging-in-Publication Data

Cole, Jill.
    California interiors / by Jill Cole.
        p.   cm.
    Includes index.
    1. Interior decoration--California--History--20th century.
    I. Title.
    NK2004.C65   1991
    729'.09794'09045--dc20   90-25799
                                                                        CIP

*CAVEAT—Information in this text is believed accurate, and will pose no
problem for the student or casual reader. However, the author was often con-
strained by information contained in signed release forms, information that
could have been in error or not included at all. Any misinformation (or lack of
information) is the result of failure in these attestations. The author has done
whatever is possible to insure accuracy.*

For information about our audio products, write us at:
Newbridge Book Clubs, 3000 Cindel Drive, Delran, NJ   08370

Color separation, printing and binding by
Toppan Printing Co. (H.K.) Ltd. Hong Kong

Typography by
TypeLink, Inc.

Printed in Hong Kong

10 9 8 7 6 5 4 3 2 1

Acknowledgments

Richard Norfolk, Pacific Design Center

Carolyn Reinmiller

Joel Curtis, Leo Martinez, Dennis Takeda,
Frank Goguen and Paul Shaevitz

Table of Contents

Introduction

I love California! It's October and, as I sit here in my office near the beach beginning to collect my thoughts on *California Interiors*, it's 90 degrees and the sun is shining brightly. How lucky we are, blessed with the benefits of a benevolent climate.

We are also living in a new cultural center, a place that has become known worldwide for its creative energy and innovation. From cooking to theater to fashion to fine art, each discipline influences the others. The architectural and interior design community here has certainly flourished in this new, exciting atmosphere. In turn, we local designers have exported our philosophy to other parts of the world.

What exemplifies the "California look"? I hesitate to admit that the avocado and gold (sixties), rust and brown (seventies), and peach and turquoise scheme of the eighties probably qualifies! Worse yet is the terrible, secret knowledge that this cliched color scheme was overused here more than anywhere else!

On the positive side, however, our lack of a common past frees us from the ponderous bonds of awe for what has gone before and from taking ourselves too seriously. We do not have to deal with the historical baggage that weighs down designers in more traditional locales.

Other than the occasional earthquake, our buildings do not have to withstand rigorous climes. While the rest of the country is draping itself and its windows in multiple layers for warmth and protection from the elements, we Californians are trying ever more innovative ways of exposing more of our well-toned flesh or our vast expanses of glass.

Californians have always been innovators and mavericks. Mr. Levi and his famous trousers typify the very essence of California design—simple, practical, casual, and beautiful. The fact that blue jeans are now even made by the French haute couture and worn by everyone in the world, from ditch digger to dictator, is a credit to the sensibility of our informal lifestyle. There is no doubt this move away from stuffy traditionalism and formality has been, in great part, influenced by the California lifestyle.

To us, paring down to the bare essentials comes as second nature. Eliminating the extraneous in all disciplines is nearly an unwritten law. To present, in all seriousness, one perfectly sliced strawberry on an oversized plate, with only a well-chosen mint sprig as garnish, is acceptable and nearly a religious experience in many acclaimed local dining rooms. This quaint practice, which was ridiculed for years, has begun to be imitated far afield—not only for its esthetic attributes, but also because people have come to recognize that it is a healthier way of eating.

The recent universal popularity of "California Cuisine" is not surprising at all in view of the current fitness craze. With everything from beverages to pizza being promoted with the cachet of our golden label, even the natives aren't immune to the hype. We have all learned to appreciate our eclectic cuisine as a true regional style employing Oriental, Latin, European, and American flavors with a dash of tofu and oat bran for the health conscious.

So, too, the interior designer has been influenced by this trend mixing dissimilar styles and textures to create a new design vocabulary. Many of us have been able to capitalize on the current popularity of California as icon. What is appealing about California Interiors? They are not homogenous at all; rather, they possess an attitude that is casual and uncluttered. The look of spaces can be contemporary or traditional, but they share an openness and consciousness of light and comfort. It is commonly held that, if one lives and practices here, one can intuitively recreate this feeling elsewhere. Repeatedly, fellow designers recount tales of being sent to far-flung locales for the sole purpose of reproducing a slice of California for some tycoon or maharajah. The temptation for me to include photographs of some of these exotic experiments in this book was great. However, after much deliberation, I opted for only the genuine article.

What the reader may find interesting about the projects that have been included is that they bear little visual similarity to one another. However, they do share this essential "California-ism" I have tried to describe. Hopefully, they will also give the reader some idea of the creativity we are presently enjoying here.

Only the perspective of time will tell us whether California has fostered a new and lasting style. While we wait for the answer, I'm putting on my roller skates and going for a turn on the boardwalk! Hope you enjoy the book as much as I enjoyed working on it!

Jill Cole
Marina del Rey, California

PROJECTS

Carmen Farnum Igonda Design

ALMAR CARPETS INTERNATIONAL

Principal Designers: Josephine Carmen and Clara Igonda
Graphic Designer: Valentina Lawrence
Photographer: Alex Vertikoff

Almar Carpets' new trade showroom needed to make a strong, immediate impression on a street heavily populated by the interior design industry. The 2800-square-foot location had the space, but not the necessary form or dimension to attract attention. To create a strong impression, the designers updated the exterior (the budget required a reworking rather than a replacing) with a new door and transom panel of marine-varnished rotary cut birch and a lead-faced sign. Selected outside materials are mirrored inside. The interior consists of contrasting curvilinear forms with the existing angular shapes of the space, using the set back mezzanine level above the front half of the ground floor as a starting point. An undulating wall softens this rigid shape and is echoed in the wall line, marked by the drywall ceiling detail and the junction between the woodblock floor with a carved and stitched pattern and a custom wool carpet.

This divides the entrance and display area from the rest of the ground floor. Square glazed windows pierce the undulating mezzanine wall, allowing more light, and is also repeated in the interior conference room downstairs. Lighting and artwork were chosen for their function rather than their design statement.

◄

The angled display racks on the showroom floor provide maximum visibility. The raised drywall ceiling with spotlights follows the same angled shapes.

The private offices on the mezzanine carry out the curvilinear and angular juxtaposition. The square glazed windows permit natural light from the storefront window and a view of the showroom below.

Detail of the window treatment.

The reception area immediately conveys the design concept of the showroom, from the custom designed rotary cut birch plywood desk to the lead wall plaque with gold, silver and bronze letters that spell out the client's name in an unconventional style.

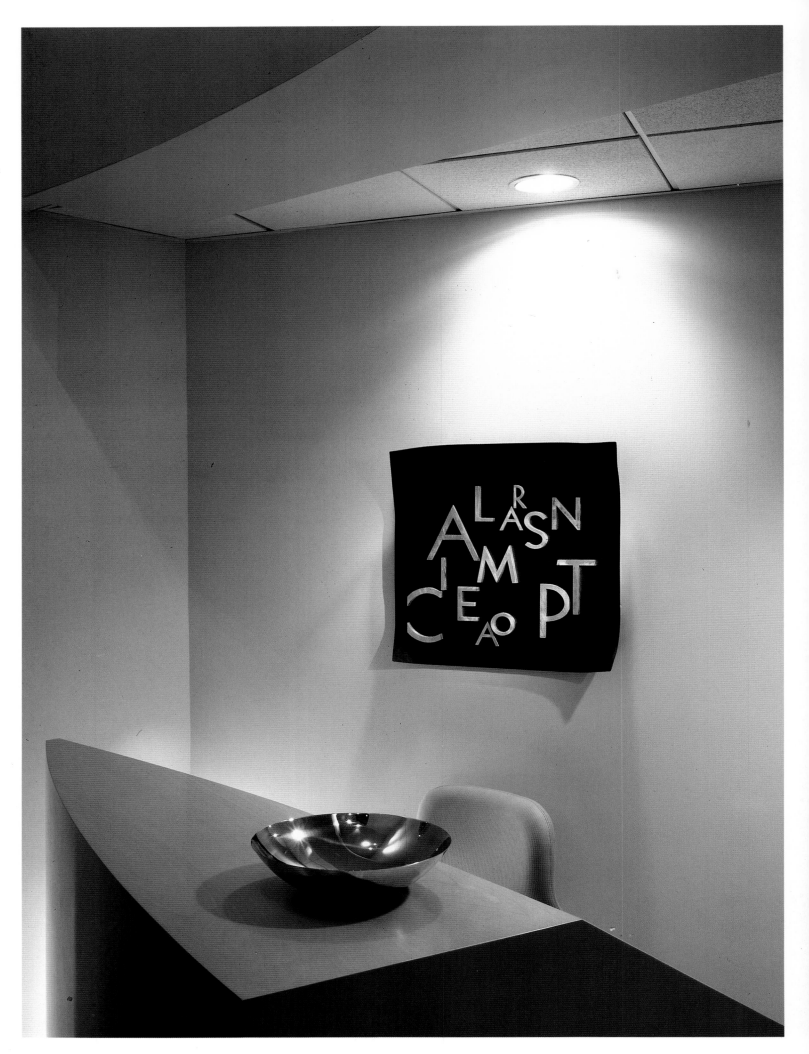

Artwork was chosen to add accent rather than make a bold statement, as in this simple silver bowl.

Detail of the wall plaque.

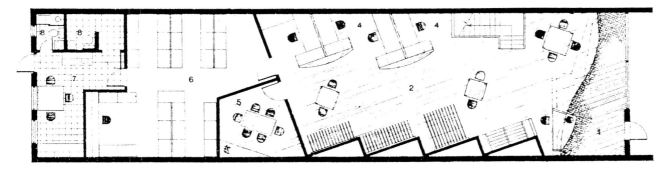

FIRST FLOOR

MEZZANINE LEVEL

Charles Gruwell Design

CIBO–RISTORANTE ITALIANO

Project Location: **Monterey, CA**
Design Director: **Charles Gruwell**
Design Associate: **Kathy Meyers**
Photographer: **Patrick Barta**
Awards: **1990 Gold Key Award, sponsored by the American Hotel/Motel Association**

Cibo Ristorante Italiano was designed to be an inviting home for generations of recipes of a very special Italian family, the Catalanos. It needed to be warm and comfortable yet current and stylish; most importantly, it needed to convey the rustic flavor of Italy.

From a white, minimal, contemporary setting, the designer began the conversion by establishing the idea of the "portico" arch which became the central unifying element throughout the restaurant and cocktail lounge. This soft arch began to paint a picture of the theme which became intensified when the walls and ceilings were completed. Plaster surfaces with an Old World finish were achieved by painting them "camel," then rubbing a terra cotta glaze over them to create a glowing yet cozy effect. The resulting texture and color reflects the rich earthen tones associated with Italy, particularly Tuscany. The floor treatment is predominantly black marble tile. In the dining areas, this is covered by an Aegean blue-green with aubergine border carpet, and in the cocktail lounge by a tapestry-inspired carpet to continue the deep, rich color palette.

The dining room chairs fit this setting perfectly, their simple and rustic shape echoes the portico arch. The chairs and banquettes are covered in a woven floral tapestry design with complementary colors. Architectural artwork is set in simple, classical frames to play up the Neo-Classical columns and Roman architectural building elements.

There's an attention to every detail, as in the terra cotta wall sconces and the footed urns.

The cocktail lounge uses a wide range of materials and textures, all in keeping with a Tuscan palette.

The discretely spotlighted dried flowers and Manzanita branches in Romanesque planters, and the uplighted trees contribute to the rustic and cozy atmosphere of one of the dining areas.

21

*Low-voltage spotlights effect the perfect balance,
ensuring Cibo's glow.*

The display kitchen adds to the rustic Italian feeling, while also being modern and efficient.

The beautiful black marble and brass bar provides the main draw of the cocktail lounge.

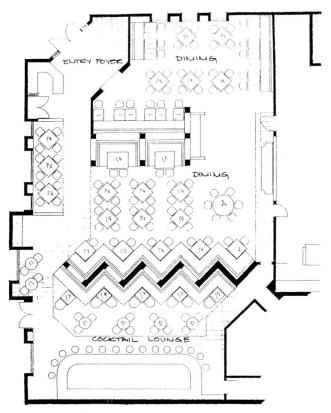

This gilded Italian mirror, an heirloom from the personal collection of the Catalano family, provides a touch of drama.

The Design Corps

WESTWOOD CONDO

Project Location: **Los Angeles, CA**
Design Team: **Leslie Harris, principal**
Etched glass wall artist: **Greg Higgins**
Photographers: **Donatella Brun, Leslie Harris**

This 2500-square-foot condo in Westwood was to be a second home for a Santa Barbara couple who came into Los Angeles three days out of the week. The space was also to function as an office. The clients were most concerned with having the duplex designed as a backdrop to part of their extensive art collection; they had chosen only works by Southern California artists for this pied-a-terre.

Furniture became an important part of the design statement, as it had to work with and complement the art, not overwhelm or compete for display. There were also budgetary considerations which were helped by reusing and re-upholstering some of the clients' existing furniture.

Another problem was the need to convert the dining room on the ground floor into a secretary's office. The difficulty of concealing this was overcome by the installation of a large acid-etched glass wall with a door by California artist Greg Higgins—a perfect solution given the couple's requirements. It concealed the office yet allowed for light to come through. It also acts as a piece of art that fits into the overall design scheme.

BUSINESS REPLY MAIL

FIRST CLASS MAIL   PERMIT NO. 37   GLEN COVE, N.Y.

POSTAGE WILL BE PAID BY ADDRESSEE

PBC International, Inc.
Mail-Order Division
One School Street
Glen Cove, NY 11542

NO POSTAGE
NECESSARY
IF MAILED
IN THE
UNITED STATES

I am interested in learning more about the books you produce for designers. Please send me more information.

Areas of interest:

☐ Architecture
☐ Fashion
☐ Graphics
☐ Hospitality
☐ Illustration

☐ Interior Design
☐ Landscape
☐ Lighting
☐ Marketing / Advertising
☐ Packaging

☐ Product
☐ Renovations
☐ Retail
☐ Sales / Promotional
☐ Other _____

NAME _____

COMPANY _____

ADDRESS _____

CITY / STATE _____ ZIP _____

COUNTRY _____

Lady Flier! Amelia Earhart, circa 1930, in classic leath

This acid-etched glass wall and door is by Los Angeles artist Greg Higgins.

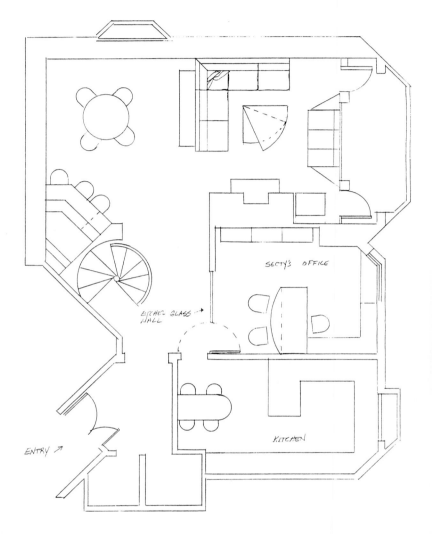

The table and chairs in the living room is also used for dining, now that the old dining area has been converted into office space.

Detail of the acid-etched glass.

29

The bronze ceramic wall sculpture is by Mary
Corse and the three-dimensional sculpture is by
Fred Fehlau.

Detail of the spiral staircase.

The furniture seems rather large from this angle, but its size juxtaposes nicely with the soaring height of the ceiling.

The living area seen from another perspective.

The Design Corps

SANTA MONICA BATHROOMS

Project Location: **Santa Monica, CA**
Design Team: **Leslie Harris of The Design Corps and Martin Gantman of Martin Gantman Studio**
Architects: **Martin Gantman Studio**
Photographer: **Ave Pildas and Charlie Daniels**

The clients needed to convert their existing bathroom and a long, narrow space that used to be a porch into a set of his-and-her bathrooms. A section of the old bathroom was converted into a walk-in closet, leaving an L-shaped room for his bathroom; she needed her space to be a combination bathroom and home office.

The material palette for his bathroom was a combination of marble grid and marble slab. The slab is inlaid flush with the plaster, except when it is an intentional part of the design statement, as in the bench in the steam shower. This same bench helped overcome other design obstacles. It helped conceal a heating duct exposed by the reconfiguration and, as a continuation of the bathroom counter around the corner, it gave a flow to the L-shaped space. The window, which looks directly on to the neighbors' house, was acid-etched, allowing light, privacy and a decorative element.

Etched glass also solves similar problems of light and privacy in her space. A door of wood and clear and etched glass was designed to separate the home office from the bathing area. The window over the closed-in bathroom, in clear, etched and cobalt blue glass, echoes the door, giving a feeling of design continuity.

The combination of clear, etched and cobalt blue glass allows the interplay of light and privacy.

Views of the area before renovation.

The bathing area was enclosed to break the planes and create private places in her bathroom.

The grid system, in the window divisions and tile pattern, unify the design and is contrasted by the oval bathtub.

Detail of the etched glass and wood door that separates her home office from her bathroom.

35

The bathroom counter continues around the corner of the L-shaped room into a marble bench in the steam shower in his bathroom.

Marble is inlaid throughout for texture rather than for mass.

The marble bench added a practical element by covering up the heating duct.

Etched glass covers up the view of the neighbor's house from his bathroom. This choice is both decorative and functional.

Two different grades of marble are creatively inlaid against each other providing a subtle design detail in his bathroom.

Goodman/Charlton Design

KALODNER RESIDENCE

Project Location: **Hollywood Hills, Los Angeles, CA**
Client: **John Kalodner**
Design Team: **Jeffrey Goodman and Steven Charlton, partners**

The client had seemingly contradictory ideas about how the interior design of his 6000-square-foot house in the Hollywood Hills should be executed. He wanted the house to remain open and airy and the spaces to be spare, orderly and uncluttered. At the same time, he wanted the overall effect to be colorful, unusual and very bold. The designers smoothed out the contradiction by choosing to create design interest by treating each piece of furniture as an individual artistic statement while keeping the overall background neutral. With the exception of a few pieces, all the furniture and artwork was custom designed, executed and hand-finished by the designers.

To keep the home uncluttered, some of the furniture also functions as artwork. For example, the massive sculptural column in the living room rotates easily on a center mechanism and converts to a media entertainment unit. This stack of equipment needs only to be seen when in use. Also, the sculpture over the bed in the master bedroom has two concealed halogen reading lights, allowing the side tables to be kept clear, and the carefully composed bed design to remain pure.

The living area effects a balance between bold and graphic and clean and restrained.

Combinations of art and function: the three-dimensional fireplace structure is visually pleasing and the tower structure reveals itself as an entertainment center.

The stark background and the streamlined design keeps the granite textures from being massive and overwhelming.

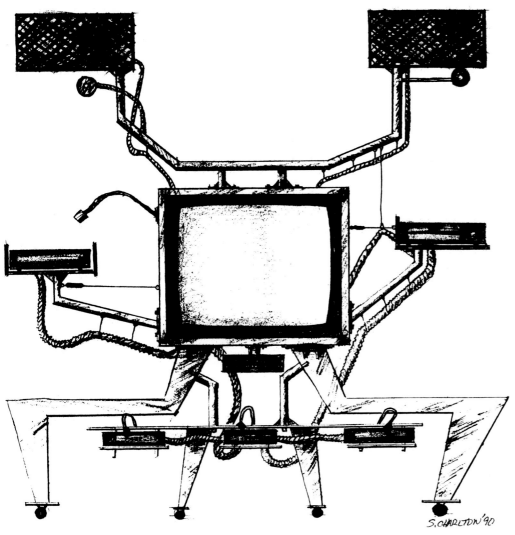

Proposed media unit for the fitness room.

Another media unit, this time cleverly tucked away over cleverly designed stainless steel shelves.

43

It's almost as if this side table is just a trompe l'oeil effect.

This minimal, yet graphic bench graces the foyer; Its shapes are echoed interestingly by the wood parquet floor.

The carpet in the master bedroom seems so three dimensional that it fulfills the visual function of furniture. The sculpture over the bed contains two halogen lamps.

Hirsch/Bedner & Associates

PARK HYATT AT THE EMBARCADERO CENTER

Project Location:	**San Francisco, CA**
Client:	**Hyatt Hotel Corp.**
Principal Designer:	**Michael Bedner**
Senior Design Associate:	**Lisa Janigian**
Project Designer:	**Timothy Zebrowski**
Architects:	**John Portman & Associates**
Photographer:	**Jaime Ardiles-Arce**

The Park Hyatt chain is renowned for their intimate, European style hotels with a reputation for personalized service and residential ambiance. The designers wanted to live up to this tradition and incorporate their own main philosophy: design arises from the character of the setting, within the commercial architectural traditions of the Embarcadero Center in the modern, yet tradition-based city of San Francisco.

The design challenge was met by using strong materials and simple lines to compliment the architecture, while contrasting it with fine details and rich surfaces. Amber-toned Australian lace-wood panelling, polished Italian granite, handmade, custom-designed carpets from China and opalescent Spanish alabaster chandeliers present a rich backdrop as a dramatic counterpoint to the classic John Portman architecture.

The designers chose a brave new mix of styles. Biedermeier, Avant-garde Italian and Classic Modern influences are reflected in Corbusier seating, high-tech lighting and fine antiques. Major Bay Area artists are represented throughout the hotel. Oriental carpet patterns, as well as traditional marquetry and dentil moldings, were contemporized to enhance the play of styles. Sensuous leathers and rich jewel tones are accented by black and gold to unify the elements in a sophisticated blend of colors, patterns and finishes. The design elements extend beyond the public areas into the 360 guestrooms and suites.

The reception area reflects the brave new mix of styles.

A view of the elevator lobby.

*Imaginative yet understated, the Park Hyatt
indulges its guests in sophisticated comfort.*

Numerous eclectic contrasts abound in the library/game room.

The suites and guestrooms contain the same design elements visible throughout the entire hotel, offering a sophisticated continuity.

Hoffman · White + Associates

MALIBU RESIDENCE

Project Location:	**Malibu, CA**
Design Team:	**Hoffman · White + Associates**
	Ellen Hoffman, Principal
	Sharon White, Principal
	Sharon Berkelo, Senior Designer
Architects:	**Choate Associates**
	Peter Choate, Partner
	Richard Blumenberg, A.I.A.
General Contractor:	**G.D. Webb Construction**
Stone Fabricator:	**Renaissance Marble**
Cabinetry:	**Poggenpohl**
	TGB Designs
Wood Flooring:	**E&P Hardwood Floors**
Lighting Consultants:	**Grenald Associates**
	Ray Grenald
	Julia Rezek
Interior/Exterior Landscape:	**Calypso**
Art Consultants:	**Hunsaker/Schlesinger**
Photographer:	**Toshi Yoshimi**

*T*his Malibu beachfront three-level residence with a rooftop sun deck and two balconies is on a narrow irregular lot with an incredible 180° view of the water but had all the disadvantages of the area: typical harsh ocean elements, traffic noise from the Pacific Coast Highway, and minimal set backs from adjacent neighbors, and the consequential lack of privacy. By designing the project with the view oriented to the ocean, and by using glass block and opaque glass to reduce sound transmission and to maximize privacy, many of these problems were effectively solved.

The client desired a clean, stark space to function as a showcase environment for their substantial art collection. The 5100-square-foot open plan was created by using all custom furniture and cabinetry, to optimize the living space in both form and function. The materials used, such as tile, plaster and glass, were chosen for their function and easy maintenance, as well as their

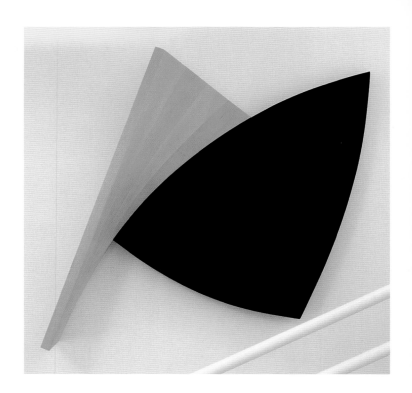

A view of the gallery on the second level—the stark white walls and the natural maple floors do not detract attention from the art.

There is a faultless symmetry in every detail.

1. ENTRY
2. GARAGE
3. MASTER BATHROOM
4. CLOSET
5. MASTER BEDROOM
6. BALCONY
7. GALLERY
8. BATH 1
9. BEDROOM 1
10. BATH 2
11. BEDROOM 2
12. KITCHEN
13. DINING AREA
14. LIVING AREA
15. BALCONY
16. SUN DECK
17. SERVICE AREA
18. ELECTRIC TRAIN SET

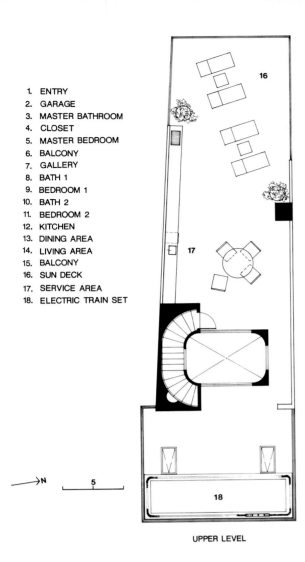

UPPER LEVEL

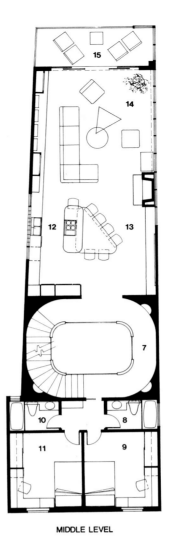

MIDDLE LEVEL

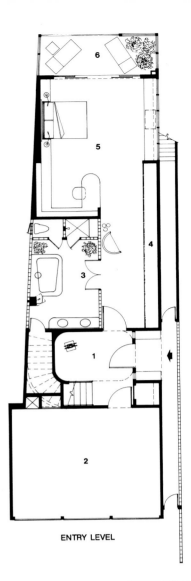

ENTRY LEVEL

The graphic No Smoking sign at the entrance matches the graphic simplicity of the total design concept.

This view of the rooftop sun deck shows two of the obstacles overcome by the house design: the narrowness of the lot and the closeness of the neighbors.

*All furniture and cabinetry were custom designed
to maximize space and function.*

Less space was alloted for the living area, dining room and kitchen combined than for the master bedroom suite.

After the dramatic starkness of the rest of the house, the granite tile and the foliage give the master bathroom a cozier, more inviting feeling.

The artwork and the view save the master bedroom from a monochromatic atmosphere.

The opaque glass allows light to filter through without relinquishing any privacy.

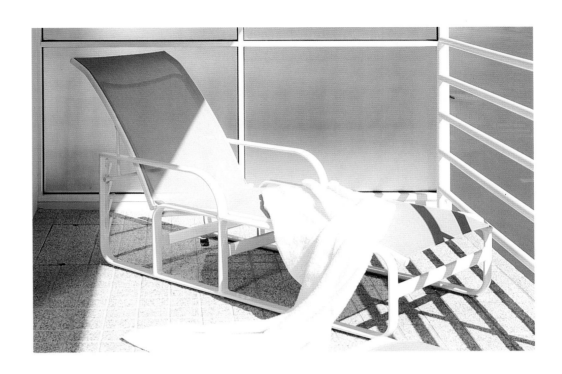

Holzbog Matloob & Associates

AKUTO

Project Location: **Los Angeles, CA**
Clients: **Francois Louie and Joel Soltanian**
Designer: **Faramarz Matloob**
Photographer: **Fay Sveltz**

The immediate impression of this upscale men's clothing boutique is that of a theatrical stage set. This dramatic setting, with its massive plaster structures simulating some neo-primitive town, enhances the elegance and stylishness of the clothes it contains. The theatrical feeling can be attributed in part to the split level of the space. The front half of the store is 30 inches lower than the back half. This posed a design problem that was overcome by the ramp. This ramp became the creative connection between the two levels and, at the same time, functions as a display area. Other display units and tables are the only mobile elements in the space excepting, of course, the merchandise.

The lighting contributes its dramatic touch. Recessed fluorescent lights cast a glow to the upper reaches. Halogen lamps reach down to illuminate the selling space, augmented by quartz light fixtures mounted on the structure.

*Display units and tables are the only movable
elements of this store.*

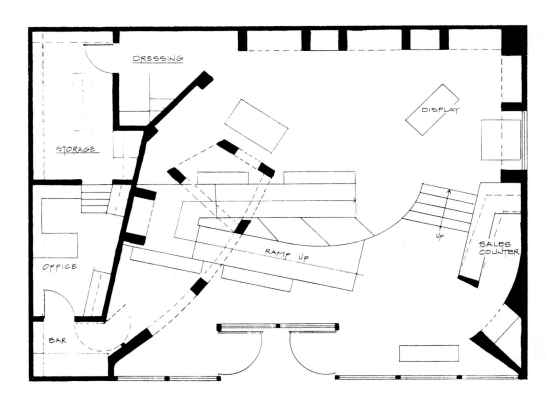

*The full effect resembles that of a dramatic stage
setting.*

The ramp functions as a means to connect the split level while serving as a display area.

The elegance of the clothes contrast with the massive plaster structures.

Another view of the ramp.

Quartz fixtures illuminate the selling areas.

The sales desk is tucked within its own stucco structure.

67

Imaginings Interior Design

EUREKA RESTAURANT AND BREWERY

Project Location:	**West Los Angeles, CA**
Project Design and Interiors:	**Barbara Lazaroff, Imaginings Interior Design**
Metal Fabrication:	**Venice Glass, Ali Harati**
Ceramic Tiles:	**Mike Payne + Associates**
Glass Block Etching:	**Polly Gessel**
Lighting Design	**Barbara Lazaroff**
Lighting System:	**Grau System and Ingo Maurer**
Kitchen Design:	**Wolfgang Puck, Barbara Lazaroff and Avery Kitchen Supply**

Designing a restaurant within a working brewery posed a unique challenge. The concept of the traditional European "pub" was rejected outright as inappropriate for the targeted clientele. It had to attract women as well as men, the gourmet diner as well as the casual beer drinker. Located in an industrial park, the idea of using industrial "high-tech" was too common, yet the designer wanted to retain the industrial feeling of the space. Five elements were chosen: various metals, imaginative tiles, artistic glass block, dramatic lighting and uniquely commissioned art. Eschewing the use of exposed ceilings and brightly painted ducts, the resulting design statement the designer calls "neo-industrial."

The metals include galvanized metal, copper, stainless steel, perforated pewter and brass. A ceramic artist, Mike Payne, was commissioned to create tiles in the form of gears and sausages. Polly Gessel was commissioned to etch glass block with gears, rivets, levers and other industrial objects. The glass blocks form striking partition walls which are lit from within, providing a warm glow. Additional lighting includes unusual German cable lights from Grau, and designer Ingo Maurer, that are uniquely constructed, emulating technological art forms. The art continues the industrial theme of this modern brewery.

◄

The entry, with its industrial portioned copper and etched glass doors covered by a sweeping copper awning, makes a dramatic impact.

The brewery is situated in an industrial park. The three protruding stacks are from the enormous brewkettles inside.

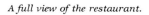

A full view of the restaurant.

In fine detail: notice the unusual German cable lights from Grau System and Ingo Maurer and the Cappellini "Xan" chairs with the chrome and cherrywood frames.

This showcase exhibition kitchen was designed by Barbara Lazaroff and Wolfgang Puck.

The counter of the exhibition kitchen is framed with slate shaped in the form of sawtooth gears.

Sausage-shaped tiles by Mike Payne line the window of the charcuterie where homemade sausages, salamis and prosciuttos are aged.

A view of the neo-industrial dining room.

This computer-driven animated steel sculpture is a folk-art relief map of Los Angeles fabricated by Cinnabar.

Texas artisan Polly Gessel was commissioned to create the etched glass block with gears, rivets, levers and other industrial objects.

R. Lee White's 10' × 10' structural relief painting is entitled "A Drop in the Bucket."

One of the three large brewkettles.

The bar has a 40-foot-long hammered copper top. Its front face is accented by perforated pewter panels with copper pipes and oversized stainless steel nuts and brass bolts. The brewkettles can be seen behind the bar.

Mike Payne created the gear-shaped ceramic tiles that accent the bathrooms and the exhibition kitchen.

International Interiors

DAUER RESIDENCE

Project Location: **Beverly Hills, CA**
Client: **Mr. and Mrs. Roger Dauer**
Interior Design: **Roy Sklarin**
Project Supervisor: **Rod Sellard**
Contractor: **Zigman Construction**
Electrician: **Ron Mogab**
Photography: **Zanzinger Productions**

The clients wanted their indoor racquetball court, a space measuring 42 × 22 feet with no windows except those of the screening room high above it, converted into a ballroom. Their only requirement was that it be totally original.

Using the theme of Hollywood in its heyday, the design was patterned after a luxurious garden penthouse overlooking the city lights. The windows were redesigned with glass block, forming the balconies. The screening room itself whimsically suggests sitting in the back seat of a Fifties roadster at a country drive-in theater.

For the ballroom, mirrors cover the bottom half of the walls, making the space seem huge and spacious. They're topped with planters filled with lush overhanging vegetation. Over the mirrors and plants, a Hollywood skyscape featuring famous landmarks was painted, using day-glo colors to accentuate the mural. When the discretely placed black lighting is turned on, the effect is stunningly three-dimensional. Three hundred "star" lights were inserted into the cobalt blue ceiling. A stage of glass block was built against one wall. Another wall was opened up with bevelled glass French doors that lead to an inner courtyard. The tables and chairs to seat 80 are of acrylic, which was more appropriate than any more substantial material. The only furniture of real weight and substance is the burgundy granite and mirrored glass bar.

*The inspiration for this converted indoor racquet-
ball court is Hollywood in its heyday.*

It's just like being in the back seat of a car at your neighborhood drive in movie.

While the guests downstairs party in an ultra-glamorous Hollywood scene, the screening room upstairs evokes more innocent, bucolic times.

81

J. Timothy Felchlin,
A.I.A.

MILLER/MAGEE RESIDENCE

Location: **Los Angeles, CA**
Principal Designer: **Tim Felchlin**
Construction Supervision: **Shinji Igozaki**
Photography: **David Glomb**

The basic organizing concept for the renovation of a small, dark and tight house with several difficult to use rooms was to create an overall container and to place within it a variety of forms to serve the functions of the client. In addition to opening up the space, a second-story study, bedroom and bath were to be added. The overall design inspiration came from the Southwestern landscapes enjoyed by the clients. The living area was raised to 18 feet to maximize volume. Its outer walls and ceiling are painted white and pierced with windows and skylights with regular openings for specific views and random openings to capture light. Within the living area, a variety of shapes house the bathroom, kitchen, study stereo cabinet, fireplace and stairwell. These shapes are defined by Painted Desert inspired colors. The entry hall, library and guest bedroom are found in the spaces between the living area container walls and the forms within it. In moving in and around the forms, one finds variety and changing perceptions. The resulting experience is both wide open and protected.

The exterior is a contrast in rough-textured and smooth stucco delineated by a large bullnose coping.

Window grille details suggest the San Andreas fault.

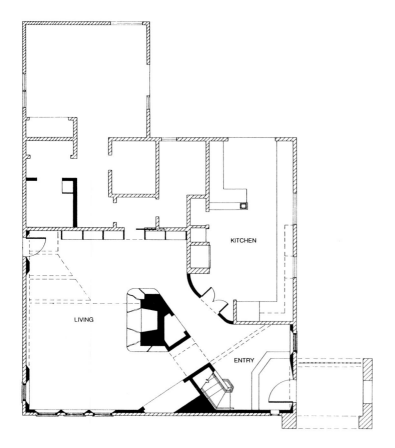

FIRST FLOOR PLAN

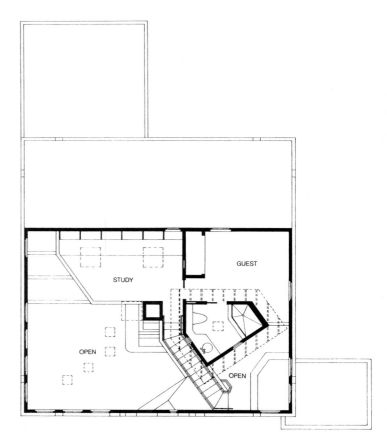

SECOND FLOOR PLAN

This sketch shows the volumetric concept of the product.

The forms and colors are inspired by the Painted Desert. The couch and chairs are Le Corbusier.

The guest bedroom is part of the second story addition contained within the living area's raised volume.

The table top is Moroccan fossil marble and the base are Frank Lloyd Wright concrete blocks.

Jain Malkin Inc.

KAISER VANDEVER CLINIC

Project Location: **San Diego, CA**
Client: **Kaiser Permanente**
Interior Design: **Jain Malkin Inc.**
Architect: **Neptune Thomas Davis**
Photographer: **Sandra Williams**
Awards: **1990 Du Pont Antron Design Award for health care design**

This project was an experiment to see if greater good would be accomplished if both the architect and the interior designer collaborated from the outset. The resulting harmonious, organized and efficient environment provided plenty of proof of true integration.

The principal consideration in the design of this 115,000 square foot, five-story space was ease with which patients and visitors could find their way around the space without getting lost. The space plan is very logical and organized, and is basically the same on each floor, which are divided into functional units longitudinally, proceeding from a public space to a greeting and processing area to the clinical area and the physicians' private offices. Each floor has a different color palette coordinated throughout the space. Visitors and patients easily understand where they are and what to expect on every floor.

Much effort was taken to keep the space from the cold and sterile atmosphere common in medical facilities. The wide use of glass allows for a feeling of spaciousness, allowing for light and views of the distant mountains and the beautiful gardens and courtyards outside. Color is applied throughout, with the boldest use in the public areas and getting more subtle as it approaches the treatment areas. Each floor has an "event" which consists of a beautiful upholstered bench, an unusual piece of artwork and a ceiling with a light cove.

Vast expanses of glass offer views and plenty of light.

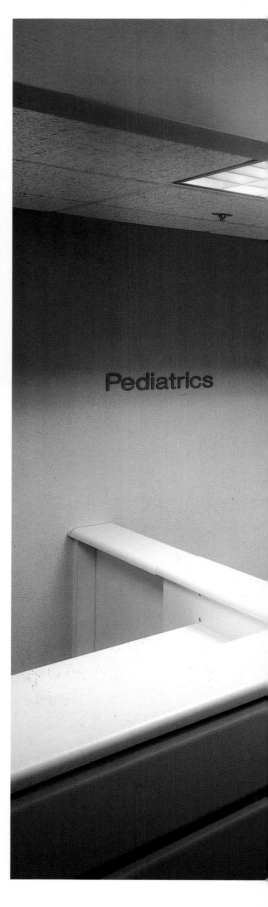

Pediatrics

Open waiting rooms on each floor flow into the public corridor, defined by the inset carpet border.

Each elevator lobby offers a dramatic view of the color palette of each floor.

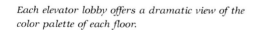

The pediatrics waiting area needed some enclosure
and the designers turned a glass wall into a giant
aquarium where the people waiting are the fish.

Jain Malkin Inc.

SCRIPPS MEMORIAL HOSPITAL

Project Location: **Encinitas, CA**
Project Manager and Chief Designer: **Linda Mitchell of Jain Malkin Inc.**
Principal Architect: **Robert Rodriguez of Brown Gimber Rodriguez Park**
Photographer: **Sandra Williams**

Encinitas needed a new healthcare facility that would be more hospitable than hospital. The community is an educated, aware one, knowledgeable in health and fitness, higher consciousness and environmentalism. Its hospital needed to be just as progressive.

The new 99,330 square foot building competes with a desert sunset for brilliance of color and drama, a far cry from stereotypical white tile monoliths. On the outside, stark stucco forms are bathed in rich hues ranging from neutral sand to terra cotta, nectarine, salmon and coral. The lobby, enclosed in a two story atrium pierced by skylights allowing natural light in, reminds the visitor of a luxury hotel. The southwestern color scheme continues on the inside, creating a warm, comfortable and inviting atmosphere.

The colors serve more than just creating the mood. They are integral part of wayfinding, the ability of patients and visitors to find their way around. The colors help identify sections, floors or wings. Geometric shapes also serve this same purpose, and also complement the overall design statement.

The lobby seems more a part of a luxury hotel than a hospital.

A mini atrium greets the visitor, part of a two-story atrium with faceted glass skylights that encloses the lobby and admitting area.

Another view of the lobby, with its intimate groupings of traditional upholstered furniture contrasting with the lofty, airy atrium.

Bold geometric shapes and bright colors are used as wayfinding cueing devices.

Bright colors and strong shapes make waiting a more pleasant experience.

This patient room is a far cry from the drab, sterile rooms of other institutions.

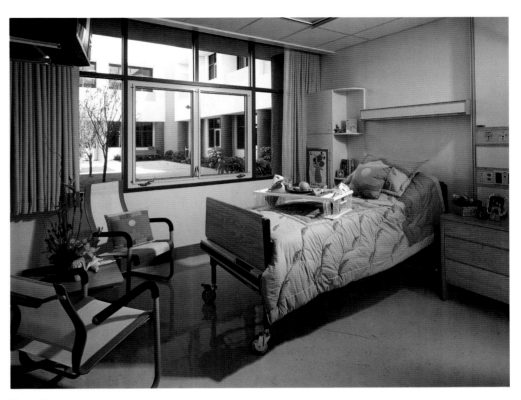

The hydrotherapy room resembles a European spa. The ceramic tile floors are intricately patterned in "area rug" designs and are complimented by the intricate borders of the ceramic tile walls.

Kirkpatrick Associates

AUDIO/VIDEO SHOWROOM

Location: **Beverly Hills, CA**
Client: **Christopher Hansen LTD.**
Audio/Video Showroom
Principal Designers: **Grant C. Kirkpatrick and Stephen B. Straughan**
Lighting Designer: **Alena Appia, Grenald Associates Ltd.**
Project Architect: **Russell Hatfield**
Project Assistants: **Rachel Dougan and Cindy Utterback**
Photographer: **David Glomb**

The existing 5400-square-foot art deco building was first made earthquakeproof then repaired and resurfaced to its original form. A new facade was inserted into the shell, reflecting the similar design and function of the esoteric merchandise that it would house: birch wood display arches, black granite banding and the juxtaposition of clear and diffused glass.

The design of the interior was developed with the focus on keeping the space clean and museum-like so that the visual excitement would be created by the merchandise, yet still offer a sense of the comforts of home. Extensive use of clear and diffused laminated glass provides adequate light yet allows for privacy and keeps out extraneous noise. Colors, materials and period furnishings were chosen to create the mood and exhibit the flexibility of the merchandise for many environments.

The colors, materials and contrasting period furnishings create a sense of home while remaining clean.

The new facade recalls the similar design and functional qualities of the merchandise inside.

The gallery has plenty of open space for flexibility.

The coffered and undulating ceilings and baffled walls utilize a variety of hard and soft materials to reflect and absorb sound waves in accordance with acoustic principles.

Detail of the display rack.

Diffused laminated glass provides light transmittance throughout while providing privacy and sound attenuation.

The design was focused on keeping the space clean and museum-like.

Another view of the gallery hall.

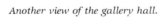

Kirkpatrick Associates

THE MANHATTAN LANTERNS

Project Location: **Manhattan Beach, CA**
Principal Designers: **Grant C. Kirkpatrick and Stephen B. Straughan**
Project Assistants: **Cindy Utterback and Michael Selditch**
Photographer: **Weldon Brewster**

The project is a speculative development consisting of three townhouses located one block from the beach. Each unit was designed to take advantage of ocean views and breezes with attention to privacy and a sense of ownership in a multi-family building.

Isolating three distinct volumes on the third floor with decks in between to capture 180° ocean views gave each unit individuality within the overall design and maximizes light and views. These volumes, intended as the living areas are enhanced by the use of clerestories floating the roofs, creating 360° diffused blue light during the day and a lantern-like illumination of the eaves at night. Clear and diffused glass are used extensively throughout, allowing both light and privacy.

Skylights over the stairs provide indirect illumination.

The Manhattan Lanterns at dusk. Note the clerestories illuminating the eaves.

108

The decks providing sweeping ocean views.

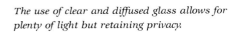
The use of clear and diffused glass allows for plenty of light but retaining privacy.

Wood floors, marble and granite counters, fireplaces and cedar ceilings provide a more spacious feel.

Marieann Green Interior Design

BEVERLY HILLS RESIDENCE

Project Location: Beverly Hills, CA
Principal Designer: Marieann Green

This remodelling project necessitated finding a balance between the rusticity of the structure and the contemporary art collection that it would house. The client required that the country feel of the home be taken only as far as in keeping with its shell and that no color should be used. The designer did not want the interior to function only as a stark gallery for the art. The balance was effected through the furnishings, making use of antiques and fine reproductions in the classical style. Worn, faded antique kilims cover the floors, softening the terra cotta tile and antique oak. Large, down-filled furniture was added to increase the comfort and tone down the hard edges. The final result is a fine juxtaposition of rusticity and sophistcation, visually pleasing and physically comfortable. There is a consistency to the overall effect without any need for compromise on the part of either the client or the designer.

From shag-pile carpeting and heavy drapery to 18th century French terra cotta tile and antique oak and plenty of light.

An inside view of the A frame: the barn siding adds to the rustic touch and the heavy, downfilled furniture softens the hard surfaces.

The designer suspects that the A-frame is a later addition by a previous owner.

The furnishings served as a bridge between the country feeling and the contemporary art. At the entry, an antique Italian settee sits beneath "Natte" by Antoni Tapies.

Detail of the dining room: the art is by Penck.

The client wanted to avoid all color so the home would function as a frame for her art collection.

A David Hockney lithograph sits over the fireplace.

*The large painting in the background is "The
Sharing of the Nameless" by Arakawa.*

The high arched, shuttered window adds an intriguing element to the bathing area.

The various textures of the material palette of the bathroom play well off each other.

Even the most pared-down, neutral environments
should be made to feel livable.

Mulder-Katkov Architecture

2 KETCH

Project Location: **Marina Del Rey, CA**
Partners-In-Charge: **Miriam Mulder and Richard Katkov**
Project Architect: **Gregory Makowski**
Photographer: **Dominique Vorillon**

The clients required a complete interior transformation of an existing 1600 square foot, bi-level condominium on the top level of a three-story building with a gorgeous view of Santa Monica Bay. The view dictated the architecture and organization of the unit's renovation. An unusual part of the design challenge was the clients' insistence that no paint be used. This led to the use of a wide range of natural materials, with gray pigmented plaster and wood, such as Baltic plywood and Douglas fir, being the main focal point of the material palette which also includes glass and granite. The coordination of the complex integration of materials required constant on-site supervision. Nearly everything in the unit was designed specifically for the project.

◄
A skylight pierces the entry hall.

*The gorgeous view of Santa Monica Bay deter-
mined the architecture of the renovation.*

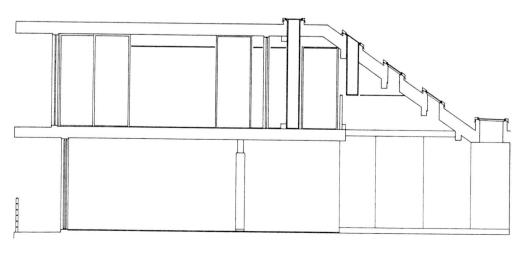

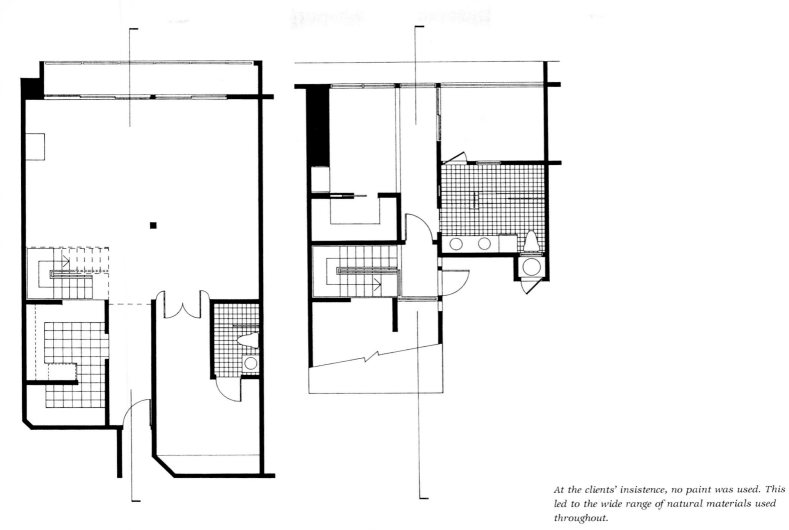

At the clients' insistence, no paint was used. This led to the wide range of natural materials used throughout.

The focal point of the design is the juxtaposition of concrete (or grey pigmented stucco) and wood.

Nearly everything, including the light sconces were designed specifically for the project.

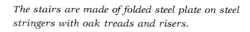
The stairs are made of folded steel plate on steel stringers with oak treads and risers.

Detail of the staircase.

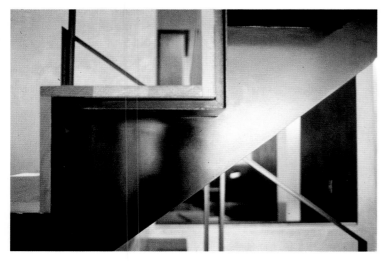

Wood contrasting wood: Baltic plywood inlays against the hardwood floor.

Detail of the living room.

The bedroom has grey pigmented plaster walls and Baltic plywood inlays in the ceiling and floors. The view dominates.

128

The bathroom is of white ceramic tile with
limestone inlays on the walls.

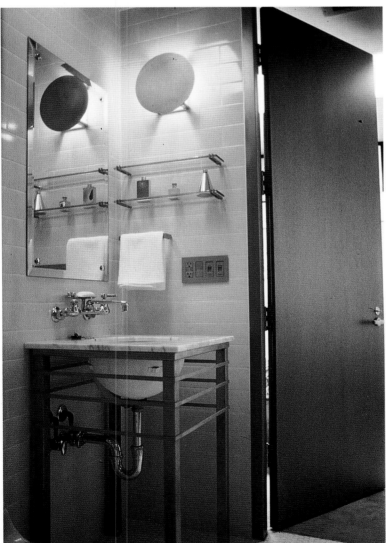

Mulder-Katkov Architecture

1611 ELECTRIC AVENUE

Project Location: **Venice, CA**
Principal in Charge of Design: **Miriam Mulder**
Principal in Charge of
Project Management: **Richard Katkov**
Project Team: **Robert Cull and Gregory Makowski**
Photographer: **Dominique Vorillon**

The designers' principal challenge was to convert a 6,000 square foot plumbing supply building into a commercial office space with a limited budget which confined them to using off-the-shelf materials. The client did allow them to conceptualize the space and delineate the interiors a little more than in most office buildings. The site is on a street marking the boundary between a working middle class residential district and a rapidly developing upscale commercial district. The designers wanted the renovation to reflect the history and context of the neighborhood. A dramatic lobby space and unusual conference room as well as other architectural elements (based on the conception of the structure as a camera obscura) take this building out of the realm of the ordinary office building.

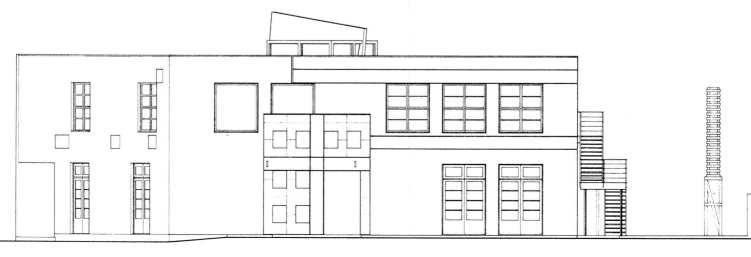

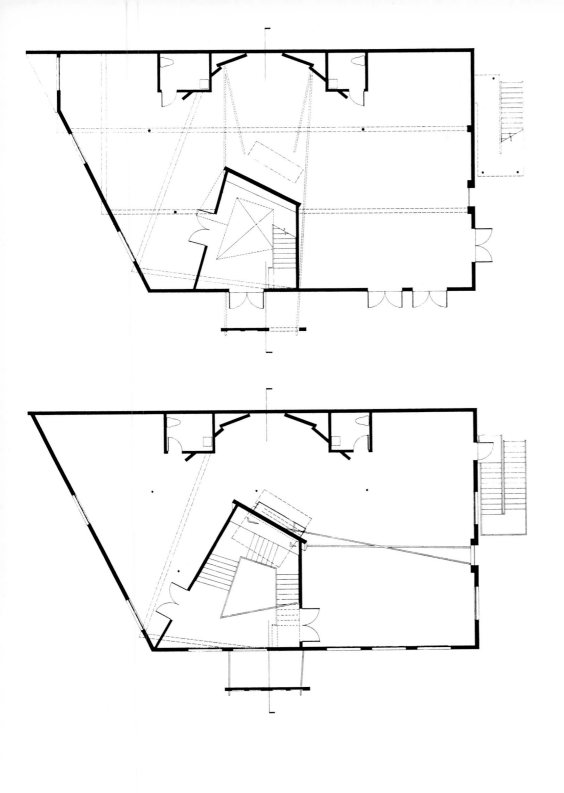

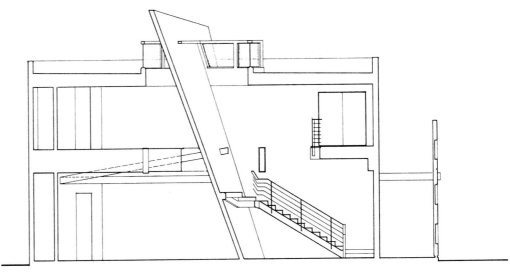

133

A view of the galvanized steel stairwell.

The free standing 16' × 15' × 8" entry screen represents a stripped-down, flattened urban wall. The 21' × 15' × 2' sculpture on the far right is a latticework box partially infilled with a metal representation of ideas reflecting the history and spirit of the neighborhood.

Phyllis Rowen Sugarman Inc.

SUGARMAN RESIDENCE

Project Location: **Beverly Hills, CA**
Client: **Louis and Phyllis Rowen Sugarman**
Principal Designer: **Phyllis Rowen Sugarman**
Draftsman: **Dean Carlson**
Design Assistants: **Allyson Rowen Taylor and Wendy G. Weiner**
Contractor: **Keith Miller**
Photographer: **Charles S. White**

The limits and challenges of working with a client did not apply in this case. The roof of the designer's original home had developed large leaks when a new air-conditioning system was installed. Planning a new roof eventually led to total renovation and expansion. The exterior was altered and given a Mediterranean facade. Caissons were built to accommodate a larger deck area (redwood gave way to flagstone), an additional story and a new breakfast room. All windows, floors and lighting changed to effect a more open floor plan. Electronics, such as stereo and intercom systems, were updated and built in.

Once the basic layout was set, it was time to refurnish the interior with their extensive and eclectic collection of antique furnishings, objects and artwork, mixed with contemporary paintings and sculpture. Rather than using the interior as a setting, the designer achieved a harmonious composition of the various and diverse elements, creating a distinct and unique home.

A late 19th century allegorical painting dominates
one wall of the living room.

The living room is an eclectic mix of Beidermeier, Regency, Louis XIV and Oriental influences.

The Aubusson tapestry and antique pillow coverings and upholstery add a soft touch to this room.

Detail of the Aubusson wall hanging and pillows.

The reproduction Regency dining room table can accommodate a wide variety of table settings.

The snake sculpture by Frank Gehry juxtaposes nicely with the undulating rug from Louis Sugarman's own firm, Rodeo Mills.

The painting is early 20th century American school, the base and platter are circa 1940 Chinese rose Canton and the console is French Empire.

Some of the pieces are the same but changing the painting and candlesticks creates a whole new mood.

The den is another eclectic mix of decorative objects and styles and features "Sin" by Ed Ruscha.

The same room with horns, without Ruscha.

The redone flagstone deck affords magnificent hillside vistas.

Artist David Urqhart painted the pool walls with a trompe l'oeil garland.

145

Antique French furnishings and decorative objects highlight the master bedroom.

Vegetation outside the French windows help screen the bather and bring nature closer inside.

147

Ridgway Associates

COUDERT BROTHERS

Project Location:	Los Angeles, CA
Client:	Coudert Brothers, Attorneys and Counsellors at Law
Principal in Charge of Design:	Patricia Ridgway
Principal in Charge of Project Management:	Thomas Pyle
Project Director:	Marc Mowery
Job Captain:	John Rauh
Photographer:	Robert Pisano Architectural Photography

The clients, an international law office whose main offices are based in Los Angeles, wanted space that would reflect the contemporary nature of their partners but would also reflect the firm's long established presence. This was accomplished by including in the design statement the California Arts and Crafts movement, highlighted by contemporary California artwork and the bold use of black bands of color which were borrowed from the firm's existing Oriental art collection.

Another requirement was to capture an ocean view when stepping from the elevator into the firm's entry lobby. This was achieved by constructing a descending connecting stair which begins on the twentieth floor, leading into an immediate landing and separating into two staircases flowing to the nineteenth floor. The descending stair allows for the viewer's sight line to see over the etched glass stair rail, through the glass window enclosing the conference room to the view beyond.

The designers chose a variety of stones such as granite, marble and French limestone as well as anigre wood veneer for their rich palette of materials. The use of a black and white banded element was boldly used at the entry and subtly repeated throughout the 36,630-square-foot space, beginning with the upholstered seating in the reception area and carried into the private offices.

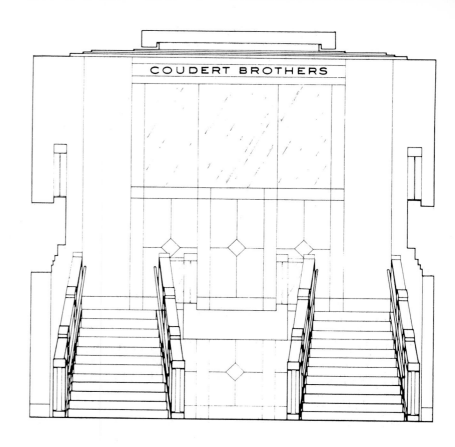

Graphic black-and-white bands are used boldly at the entry and are subtly repeated throughout.

150

A staircase descends from the twentieth floor leading to a landing.

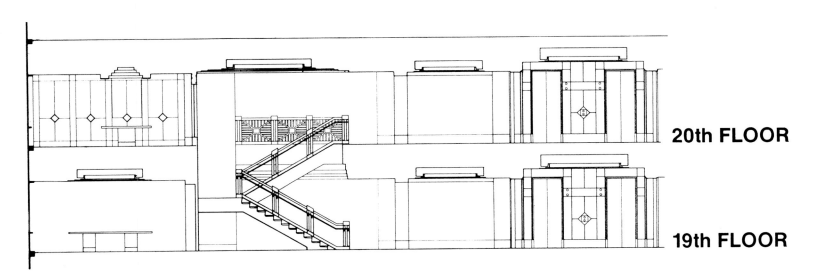

20th FLOOR

19th FLOOR

The conference table and panelled walls were custom designed with the veneers inherent reflective qualities in mind.

Contemporary California artwork graces the waiting area.

Elements from the Weiner Werkstadt can be seen in the drywall ceiling soffits and the precision of the line work in the custom designed table.

SLAB
(architects)

FIRE:LIGHT

Project Location:	**Marina Del Rey, CA**
Client:	**Norma Lynn Cutler**
Principal Designer:	**Martin Roy Mervel**
Fabricator:	**Paul Burnsweig of Metalmorphosis**
Photographer:	**Tom Bonner**

The client lived in a condominium adjacent to the beach and wanted her existing fireplace transformed by creating one of both art and function. The only practical aspects involved would be firewood storage and adequate and proper lighting of the final installation. The materials chosen were cold rolled steel, stainless steel, aluminum and glass.

A spark creates fire.
Fire destroys matter and creates heat.
When matter is destroyed new patterns arise.
Time is measured and recorded with mechanical devices.
Light is used to sketch unpredicted relationships.
Fragment and whole are addressed.
The installation is an intrusion to domestic space.
This alien is welcomed.

—*Martin Roy Mervel*

The display is discreetly illuminated and dimmed on two circuits.

Firewood storage had to be taken into account.

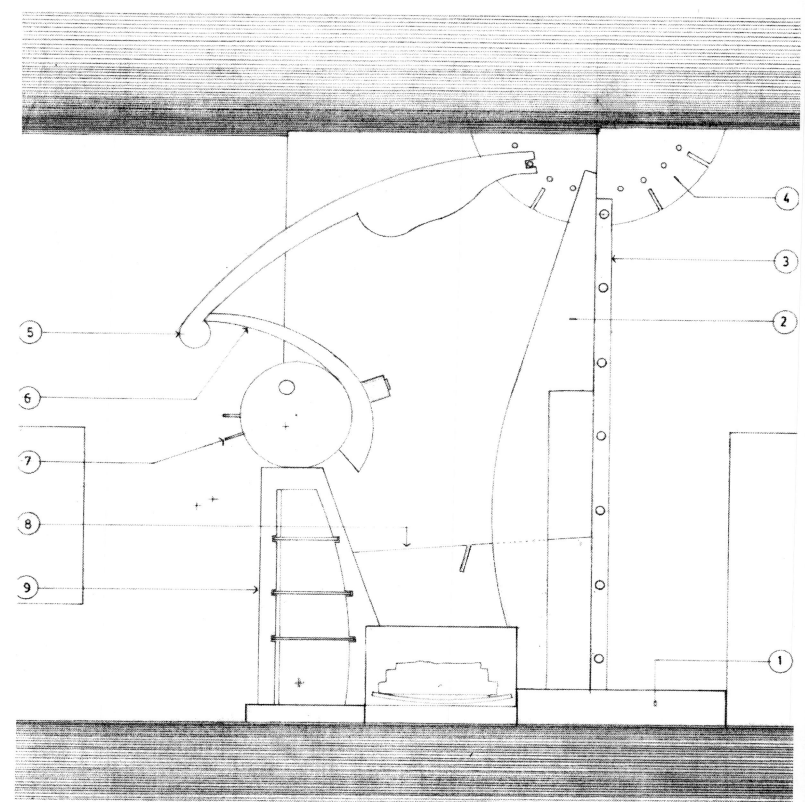

THE FIREPLACE PARTS LIST

1.   BASE   PLATFORM
2.   LOG STORAGE COLUMN
3.   HINGE
4.   TIME INSTRUMENT
5.   HAMMER
6.   REFLECTOR
7.   HEAD
8.   SMOKE PLATE
9.   DISPLAY STORAGE

This alien is welcomed.

Springfield Design

CARRERA Y CARRERA

Project Location:	**San Francisco Centre, San Francisco, CA**
Clients:	**Carrera y Carrera de Madrid and Mandarin Gems**
Project Owner:	**Paul Lam**
Architectural and Interior Design Firm:	**Springfield Design**
Project Designers:	**Jaci Springfield and Karen Strauss**
General Contractor:	**J.W. Moore Construction**
Fixture Contractor:	**Montbleau & Associates**
Lighting Designer:	**Jaci Springfield**
Faux Finisher:	**Alyson LaBlanc**
Photographer:	**Bruce Cobb**

This project is a joint venture of two jewelry retailers, one from Madrid, the other from the United States. Two lease spaces in the San Francisco Centre were combined, creating a narrow, 1400 square foot, L-shaped plan with two floor level changes. Because the two lease spaces faced different public walkways, two storefront entrances and a roll-down door that would separate the areas in case of fire were required. The store was divided into three adjoining areas: the Promenade, for Mandarin Gems, and the domed Arena and Gallery, for Carrera Y Carrera. The Gallery is curved and wraps around the Arena. The ceilings were kept high to add volume and create an illusion of grandeur.

The design of the interior had to be complimentary to the merchandise but as a background setting rather than a distraction. The atmosphere had to be comfortable and unintimidating for the mall customer, in contrast to the formal moods of Carrera Y Carrera's European stores. Warmed toned colors and materials such as Silverblue slate, French limestone, Rosa Dequesa marble, Bolivian rosewood, ebony and hand-trowelled plaster were chosen to combine with the classic arched forms and domed ceiling for an elegant yet relaxed effect.

The storefronts were designed to be inviting and unintimidating to the mall customer.

The interiors serve as a backdrop for the jewelry, not a distraction.

The high, domed ceiling of the arena adds to the feeling of gracious elegance.

163

Steve Chase Associates

CHASE RESIDENCE

Project Location: **Rancho Mirage, CA**
Client: **Steve Chase**
Designer: **Steve Chase**
Architects: **Holden and Johnson**
Photographer: **Arthur Coleman**

The designer's motto is "a maximum of architecture, a minimum of trimmings," and he is able to follow this to the limit in designing his own 10,000-square-foot home in Palm Springs. Inspired by the desert and its bizarre natural forms, he has created a home that complements its location. The material palette—granite, glass, stone, slate, onyx and tile—is massive, almost prehistoric. Yet, the result is contemporary because of the simple, classical lines that are used throughout. Pastel desert colors and abstract art augment the cross-shaped, open plan which also takes advantage of the magnificent views of the Santa Rosa mountains and the Mojave desert. Instead of gardens, cacti, palm trees, and local vegetation is utilized for plantings.

◄

The entry hall of the main house shows a Zen inspiration.

An aquarium highlights the master bathroom.

*Modern art highlights the living room. The
"Desert Storm" by the designer flashes overhead.*

Cacti and the Santa Rosa mountains surround the house.

The stone colonnade contrasts sharply against the desert night sky.

Strong, graphic shapes blend into the harsh desert landscape.

169

Cacti and the Santa Rosa mountains surround the house.

The gazebo, with its mosaic tiled chairs, provides a festive backdrop for a meal.

The sitting room of the guest house has a magnificent view of the grounds and the main house.

The material palette of the office evokes a tropical rainforest.

A glass pane partition separates the dressing room from the bathing area.

The master bedroom is filled with a variety of interesting textures.

Color and light give the guest bedroom a cozy glow.

Studio E Architects

STUDIO E ARCHITECTS OFFICE

Project Location: **San Diego, CA**
Client: **Studio E Architects**
Design Team: **Bradley Burke, Douglas Childs and Eric Naslund**
Renderer: **Teddy Cruz**
Photographer: **Ryan Roulette**
Awards: **1989 Design Award from the American Institute of Architects**

The project is a 600-square-foot space in an existing two-story warehouse in a downtown area that had recently turned into a visual arts district. It needed to be a functional and striking office that would create a signature space for a newly-formed architectural firm. With only a budget of a few hundred dollars, the project was constructed by the staff mainly after hours and late into the night. By arranging standard hardware store materials in a more sophisticated manner through careful placement and simple, clean detailing, the designers aims were achieved.

The space needed to be a striking signature for the newly formed architectural firm.

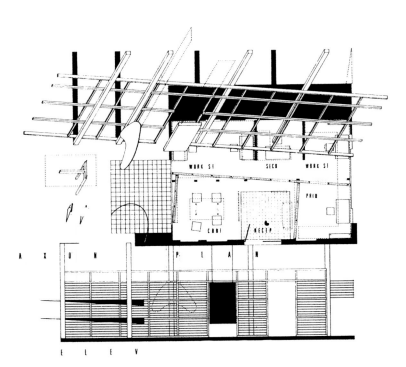

The smallness of the site necessitated the precise division of space.

The glass top of the conference table gives an illusion of spaciousness.

Details shows the careful construction by the staff.

The careful and subtle use of color enlivens the space.

Standard hardware store materials were arranged in a sophisticated manner.

Studio E Architects

SNYDER'S FLOWERS

Project Location: **San Diego, CA**
Client: **John Snyder**
Principal Designer: **John Sheehan**
Photographer: **David Harrison**

Time was of the essence in the redesign of this 1500-square-foot retail florist shop. The designers had one month from the time the lease was signed to the targeted opening date. This schedule included demolition and design time. By developing a three-dimensional model and building directly from that model, the time problem was minimized and resulted in an intensely sculptural space. The forms and shapes are massive and monolithic to sharply contrast with the delicate, ephemeral nature of the merchandise it would contain. The materials used include copper sheathing, concrete block and drywall.

The shop is divided longitudinally by a massive yellow partition, creating a work space and a sales area. A chunky stepped wall anchors the left side of the store; its form provides display opportunities as well as disguising the office tucked behind it. Centered in the arrangement is the rawly constructed concrete sales counter. "Fossils" of leaves and flowers are pressed into the countertop. The refrigerator is copper-sheathed, providing another massive, monolithic shape to contrast with the flowers.

Copper sheathing transforms the refrigerator, incorporating it into the design statement.

Snyder's Flowers is a vivid spot of color against the twilight.

The massive, monolithic forms contrast nicely with the delicate flowers.

"Fossils" of leaves and flowers are pressed into the countertop of the rawly constructed sales desk.

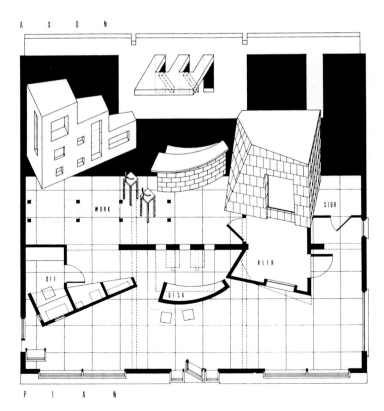

Sulana B. Sae-Onge

TROPICAL MODERN

Project Location: **La Costa, CA**
Client: **Sulana B. Sae-Onge**
Architect: **Sulana B. Sae-Onge**
Engineer: **Gerald B. Steel**
Contractor: **Halper Brothers**
Lighting: **Killian Smith of Crest Electrical**
Atrium and Mirror: **Doug Harper of Clear Cut Glass**
Koi pond and waterfalls: **Terry Hollingworth**
Horticulture: **Panya Vinotai**

This home is truly an extension of its creator. Every feature, every detail was designed especially to fit into the overall result. Through the artistic blending of the colors and textures of the glass, lead and wood, the essence of this home is captured—harmony with the elements. Nature is not left behind when you venture indoors. The house is designed around the waterfall, immediately visible through the glass wall at the back of the house, cascading over the stone terrace, through the house and outside again through the front garden, back up to the waterfall.

There are really no separate rooms in the house, except for the master bedroom. Each space flows into another, designed to create a feeling of privacy, space and communion with nature. The architecture and the interior design are intertwined for a total living environment. Nature, function and art coexist in harmony as a reflection of its creator.

The design of the carpet represents stones in the water, mountains and nature. It was created by Michael Bates from a design of the client/designer.

186

Detail of the stone mosaic of the terrace.

The landscape is a free form, terraced tropical garden.

The waterfall cascades over the stone terrace.

*The designer's home was designed around the con-
cept of the waterfall. Water, stone, sunlight and
foliage are important elements throughout.*

Water and a wide variety of stone dominate the material palette.

The Chinese characters on the pillow mean "water" and "home."

189

Contemporary forms harmonize with the natural materials.

The "Tropical Garden" room is designed to give the feeling of being in a grotto.

The water recirculates through the house, forming an integral part of the overall design.

The breakfast room sits perched behind the kitchen. The green ceramic stools are from Thailand. The kitchen countertop is of blue pearl marble, the hardest in the world.

Built-in furniture provides display areas for objects and artifacts. Notice the carved wooden Chinese lion that guards the master bedroom.

The entry way is a mixture of Oriental and Pacific
influences.

The master bedroom is the only separate room in this very open plan.

The master bath has a jacuzzi tub, steam shower and panoramic views of La Costa.

Taction Design

BREWERY LOFT/DESIGN STUDIO

Project Location: **Los Angeles, CA**
Client: **David Mocarski**
Creative Director: **David Mocarski**
Walls, Floors and Finishing: **Kit Cameron**
Loft and Utilities: **Carlson Industries**
Photographer: **Charles Imstepf**

This loft space is designed as a large piece of sculpture—integrating old and new, art and life. The greatest challenge was to take full advantage of the large cavernous warehouse and integrate it with a sense of serenity and home. The space was to be divided into two bedrooms, living room, kitchen, bath, two large walk-in closets, a design studio, two painting studios, a workshop and indoor parking.

The loft faces the Los Angeles train yards, in an old industrial area with a beautiful view of downtown. The natural light is outstanding due to four large skylights piercing the high, wood barrel vault roof. A series of open walls of different heights was constructed so as not to close off the 5000-square-foot space. A 1700-square-foot L-shaped loft was then constructed to take full advantage of the height of the space and create a series of views. A raised, Japanese-style wood floor was added in the living room and kitchen, with a spiral staircase to the loft area. The architectural elements were kept minimal in order to allow the space to interact with the light from the large windows and skylights.

This large, flexible space is left open to change. The walls have been painted in seven different color combinations. The furniture, mostly custom designed and produced by the designer/owner, is constantly changing. There is a never-ending potential for new ideas and continuous experimentation.

The loft was designed to be a flexible space open to change. It holds a never-ending potential for new ideas and continuous experimentation.

The designer's objective was to take full advantage of the huge warehouse space and integrate it with a sense of serenity and home.

A series of open walls of different heights avoids closed off space and allows light to come through.

The architectural elements were kept very minimal to let the space interact with the light.

The design studio is upstairs in the loft area. Notice the honey amber, wood barrel vault roof pierced by one of the four skylights.

UA
Design Group
BINZLEY RESIDENCE

Project Location: **Glendale, CA**
Client: **Binzley**
Vice President: **Kevin Unbehagen**
Senior Designer: **Tim Cotteriu**
Photographer: **Jeff Eichen**

*T*he restoration of this 8000 square foot, 1925 California Spanish style house, situated on 2½ acres of land, is an ongoing project. The clients could take the time to fully develop the design concept of their home in close collaboration with the designers. This association is a very important facet of this project. The result, when it is finally completed, will undeniably bear the mark of the clients' style, not of the designers. It is the latter's job to develop that style along. They are also working closely with the architects and landscapers to ensure overall continuity.

The main living area of the house has been completed. It's a large room, with one circular, tower-shaped end, that needed to be broken up into smaller cozier conversation areas. all the metal and marble furniture were custom-made in Mexico for budgetary reasons but also led to delays in delivery. Rugs had to be found to match the hand-painted tile. The clients' distinctive art and artifact collection, mostly Balinese and Asian, had to be housed but in such a way to retain the feeling that the visitor is in a comfortable home, not a museum.

Fine cobalt blue moldings highlight the oak beams and rust colored ceiling and pick up the colors of the antique rug.

The baby grand piano anchors the tower-shaped end of the living room.

All the metal and marble furniture were custom made in Mexico, including this copy of a Roman day bed.

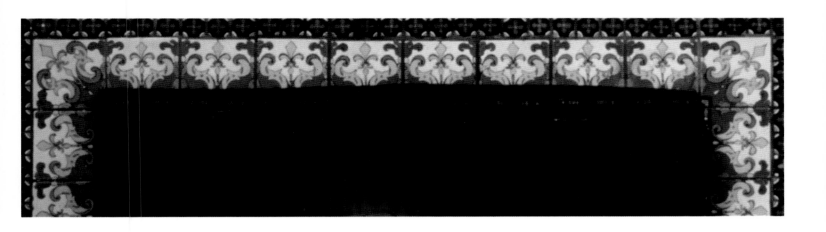

Vincent Jacquart Design Studio

KEITH RESIDENCE

Project Location: **Los Angeles, CA**
Client: **Dr. Paul Keith III**
Senior Designer: **Vincent Jacquart**
Designer: **Hubert de la Mariniere**
Assistant Designer: **Antonia Hutt**
Landscape Designer: **Robert Tainsh**
Photographer: **Marie Cosindas**

The client's property has an interesting history. It was built for and by C.R. Toberman, whose father was the last 19th century mayor of Los Angeles. Toberman built Grauman's Chinese Theater and helped develop Hollywood Boulevard. He developed Outpost estates, up in the Hollywood Hills, and built the first skyscraper in downtown LA. He used the same technique of steel and concrete to build his house on Outpost Drive. Later his home ended up in the possession of Bela Lugosi whose panther is buried on the grounds.

This 4500-square-foot colonial, with 1.7 acres of gardens, a pool house pergola and guest house, was rather difficult to update. The steel and concrete structure had steel windows and suspended plaster ceilings that created problems in installing central air-conditioning, central sound, security system, telecommunication, new electrical wiring and plumbing. Toberman, for all his foresight, did not envision the technology of the late twentieth century. Once the basics were finally installed, it was time for the designer to create the perfect home environment for his client, using furnishings that are classical, opulent and eccentric.

The living room reveals the designer's strong
Middle Eastern influences.

The use of red in this cozy room makes the room opulent, not garish.

The dining room is right out of the court of the Sun King.

212

Another view of the dining room.

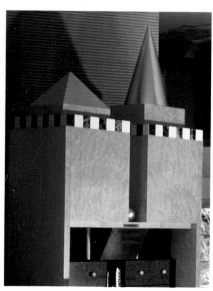

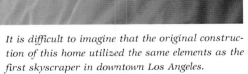

It is difficult to imagine that the original construction of this home utilized the same elements as the first skyscraper in downtown Los Angeles.

Appendix

Carmen Farnum Igonda Design
1655 N. Cherokee Ave
#300
Los Angeles, CA 90028
ATT: Josephine Carmen

Charles Gruwell Design
311 Forest Ave
Pacific Grove, CA 93950
ATT: Charles Gruwell

Design Corps, The
501 N. Alfred St
Los Angeles, CA 90048
ATT: Leslie Harris

Goodman/Charlton Design
716 N. Citrus Ave
Los Angeles, CA 90038
ATT: Steven Charlton

Hirsch/Bedner & Associates
3216 Nebraska Ave
Santa Monica, CA 90404
ATT: Lee Trout

Hoffman • White + Associates
1750 14th Street E.
Santa Monica, CA 90404
ATT: Ellen Hoffman

Holzbog Matloob & Associates
8797 Beverly Blvd
#220
Los Angeles, CA 90048
ATT: Thomas J. Holzbog

Imaginings Interior Design
805 N. Sierra Dr
Beverly Hills, CA 90210
ATT: Barbara Lazaroff

International Interiors
8500 Melrose Avenue
#204
Los Angeles, CA 90069
ATT: Roy Sklarin

J. Timothy Felchlin
8949 Sunset Blvd
#202
W. Hollywood, CA 90069

Jain Malkin Design
7606 Fay Ave
La Jolla, CA 92037

Kirkpatrick Associates/Architects
10801 National Blvd
#104
Los Angeles, CA 90064
ATT: Grant Kirkpatrick

Marieann Green Interior Design
947 N. Lacienega Blvd
#1
Los Angeles, CA 90069
ATT: Marieann Green

Mulder-Katkov Architecture
2228 Glencoe Ave
Venice, CA 90291
ATT: Miriam Mulder

Phyllis Rowen Sugarman Inc
1569 Lindacrest Dr
Beverly Hills, CA 90210
ATT: Phyllis Rowen Sugarman

Ridgway Associates
414 Boyd St
Los Angeles, CA 90013
ATT: Amy Roediger

Slab Architects
1750 N. Serrano Ave
Los Angeles, CA 90027
ATT: Martin Roy Mervel

Springfield Design
715 J Street
#305
San Diego, CA 92101
ATT: Karen Strauss

Steve Chase Associates
70-005 39th Ave
Rancho Mirage, CA 92270
ATT: Steve Chase

Studio E Architects
711 Eighth Ave
Suite E
San Diego, CA 92101
ATT: Carolyn Konzen

Sulana B. Sae-Onge
7316 Cadencia St
La Costa, CA 92009

Taction Design
621 S Avenue 21
Los Angeles, CA 90031
ATT: David Mocarski

UA Design Group
1130 6th Avenue
#248
San Diego, CA 92101
ATT: Kevin Unbehagen

Vincent Jacquart Design Studio
706 Heliotrope Dr
Los Angeles, CA 90029
ATT: Antonia Hutt

Index

ART CONSULTANT

LIGHTING CONSULTANTS

ARCHITECTS

PHOTOGRAPHERS

CLIENTS

DESIGN DIRECTOR

INTERIOR DESIGNERS

DESIGNERS